I Know Numbers/Los números

Reading consultant/Consultora de lectura:
Susan Nations, M.Ed.,
author, literacy coach,
and consultant in literacy education/
autora, tutora de alfabetización,
y consultora de desarrollo de la lectura

Please visit our web site at: www.earlyliteracy.cc
For a free color catalog describing Weekly Reader® Early Learning Library's list
of high-quality books, call 1-877-445-5824 (USA) or 1-800-387-3178 (Canada).
Weekly Reader® Early Learning Library's fax: (414) 336-0164.

Library of Congress Cataloging-in-Publication Data available upon request from publisher.
Fax (414) 336-0157 for the attention of the Publishing Records Department.

ISBN 0-8368-6485-9 (lib. bdg.)
ISBN 0-8368-6490-5 (softcover)

This edition first published in 2006 by
Weekly Reader® Early Learning Library
A Member of the WRC Media Family of Companies
330 West Olive Street, Suite 100
Milwaukee, WI 53212 USA

Editor: Dorothy L. Gibbs
Art direction: Tammy West
Cover design and page layout: Kami Strunsee
Photographer: Gregg Andersen
Translators: Tatiana Acosta and Guillermo Gutiérrez

Printed in the United States of America

1 2 3 4 5 6 7 8 9 10 09 08 07 06

Note to Educators and Parents

Learning to read is one of the most exciting and challenging things young children do. Among other skills, they are beginning to match the spoken word to print and learn directionality and print conventions. Books that are appropriate for emergent readers will incorporate many of these conventions while also being appealing and entertaining.

The books in the *I'm Ready for Math* series are designed to support young readers in the earliest stages of literacy. They will love looking at the full color photographs while also being challenged to think about and develop early math concepts. This integration allows young children to maximize their learning as they see how thoughts and ideas connect across content areas.

In addition to serving as wonderful picture books in schools, libraries, and homes, this series is specifically intended to be read within instructional small groups. The small group setting enables the teacher or other adult to provide scaffolding that will boost the reader's efforts. Children and adults alike will find these books supportive, engaging, and fun!

—Susan Nations, M.Ed., author, literacy coach,
and consultant in literacy development

Nota para los maestros y los padres

Aprender a leer es una de las actividades más emocionantes y estimulantes para los niños pequeños. Entre otras destrezas, los niños están comenzando a entender la relación entre el lenguaje oral y el escrito, y a aprender convenciones de la letra impresa como la dirección de lectura. Los libros apropiados para lectores incipientes deben incorporar muchas de estas convenciones, además de resultar atrayentes e interesantes.

Los libros de la colección *Ya puedo aprender matemáticas* están pensados para apoyar a los jóvenes lectores en las primeras etapas de ese aprendizaje. Los niños disfrutarán mirando las fotografías a todo color mientras se les invita a pensar en los primeros conceptos matemáticos y a desarrollarlos. Esta integración permite a los niños pequeños progresar en el aprendizaje, ayudándoles a entender la conexión entre conceptos e ideas de distintas materias.

Además de servir como maravillosos libros ilustrados en escuelas, bibliotecas y hogares, estos libros han sido especialmente concebidos para ser leídos en pequeños grupos de lectura guiada. El contexto de un grupo reducido permite que el maestro u otro adulto proporcione el andamiaje en el que se basarán los progresos del lector. ¡Estos libros les resultarán útiles, estimulantes y divertidos a niños y a adultos por igual!

— Susan Nations, M.Ed., autora, tutora de alfabetización,
consultora de desarrollo de la lectura

1
one
—
uno

1 bear
—
1 oso

4

2

two

—

dos

2 trucks

—

2 camiones

3

three

—

tres

3 balls

—

3 pelotas

4

four

—

cuatro

4 boats

—

4 barcos

9

nine

---

nueve

9 marbles

---

9 canicas

10

ten

—

diez

10 blocks

—

10 bloques

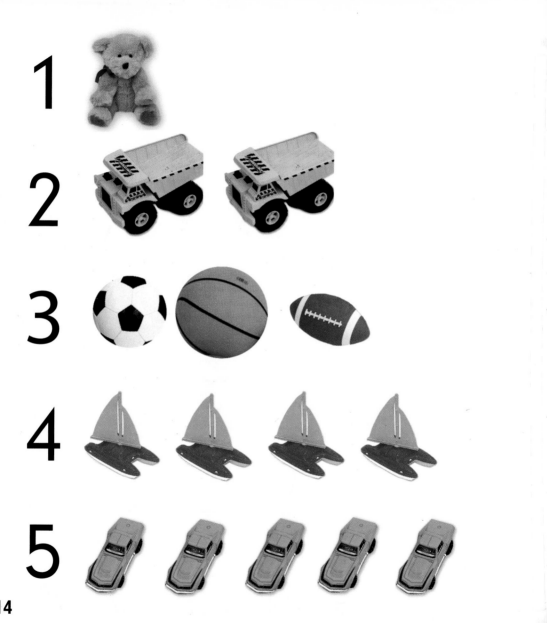

1

2

3

4

5

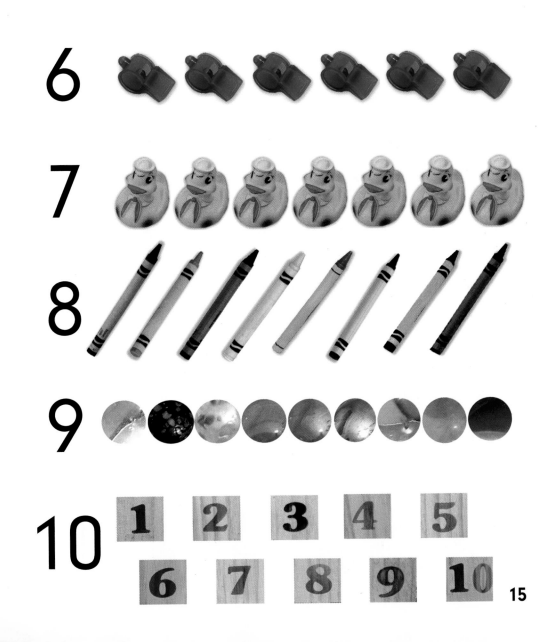

6

7

8

9

10
1 2 3 4 5
6 7 8 9 10

15

Can you name these numbers?

¿Puedes decir estos números?

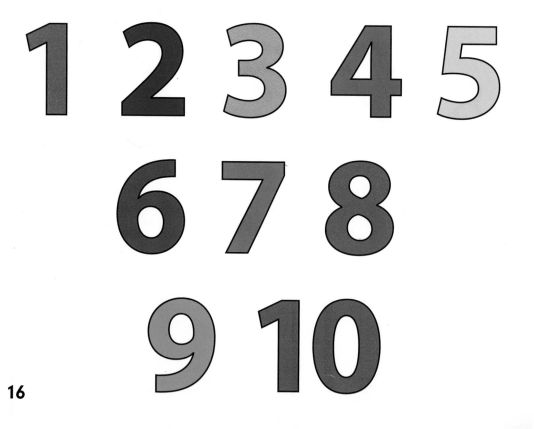